CRUDE BLACK MOLASSES

An introduction to this nutrient-packed 'wonder food', describing its beneficial effect in the treatment of a variety of ailments.

Crude
Black Molasses

Nature's Wonder Food

by Cyril Scott

ATHENE PUBLISHING CO. LTD.
Wellingborough, Northamptonshire

First published 1949
This Edition (completely revised,
enlarged and reset) 1968
Second Impression 1970
Third Impression 1970
Fourth Impression 1972
Fifth Impress (revised and reset) 1974
Sixth Impression 1976
Seventh Impression 1976
Eighth Impression 1978

AUTHOR'S NOTE

Since drawing attention to the remedial effects of
crude black molasses if taken as directed in this
booklet, molasses tablets have appeared on the
market. As the liquid, however, plays a certain
important part in the treatment, I must point out
that molasses in tablet form is unlikely to prove as
effective.

ISBN 0 7225 0241 9

Printed and bound in Great Britain
by Richard Clay (The Chaucer Press), Ltd
Bungay, Suffolk

CONTENTS

ANALYSIS OF MOLASSES

The report on a sample of molasses used in this country for making silage reveals:

	%
Sucrose	39.5
Invert sugar	11.5
Ash	9.0
Water	22.5
Organic matter	17.5

The quantity of insoluble matter is negligible. The 9 per cent ash represents soluble mineral matter largely consisting of potassium and calcium salts.

A more detailed analysis reveals the minerals iron, copper and magnesium; furthermore, that the aliment is a rich source of most of the vitamins of the B family with the exception of Vitamin B_1. According to the notable diet expert, Gayelord Hauser, it is extremely high in Vitamin B_6, in pantothenic acid and inositol; and it should be put on one's table as regularly as salt, and used as a sugar substitute on cereals, stirred into milk and eaten instead of jam or jelly.

A most important constituent of molasses is phosphoric acid: a combined deficiency of this and potassium in the human body 'causes a general breakdown of the cells, especially those of the brain and nerves.'

Crude sugar cane molasses contains about 50 per cent fruit sugars.

INTRODUCTION

Since first writing my small book on the subject some years ago, additional evidence has come to hand which goes to bear out the therapeutical value of crude black molasses if taken in the manner therein advised, therefore it would now seem appropriate that this new and more detailed edition should be compiled and made available. For after all, if there be one truth which should be emphasized in almost every book on therapeutics, it is that the *proof of the treatment is in the curing.*

And here at the outset, in case the reader may wonder why I, a layman, should ever have come to write books concerned with matters of health, the explanation is quite a simple one ... From a delicate childhood onwards I had seldom known the satisfaction of feeling really well and untroubled. Then in my early twenties I heard of nature cure, and decided to give it a trial. Even within a few days, its effect on my body, mind and spirits was so astonishingly beneficial, that it undermined my faith in medical orthodoxy — at any rate as it was at that time — and aroused in me the urge to investigate and carefully consider the claims and achievements of the *un*orthodox systems — which, as I later discovered, included homoeopathy, the (Schüssler) biochemic system of medicine, and one or two others which need not be mentioned at present.

Although the ailments from which I myself had suffered were not, so to say, 'killers' (I am now in my ninetieth year), yet it would be a strange person who did not wish to avoid what is commonly called *nerves,* that 'tired feeling', spells of deep depression, bouts of painful neuralgia, and debilitating attacks of influenza colds; all of which troubled me no longer after my conversion to naturopathy ... Granted that nowadays more people are coming, in accordance with naturopathic principles, to realize the wisdom of consuming at least a fair proportion of natural, vital foods in their daily diet; hence the increasing number of health food stores to be found in various towns. Yet the folk who patronize them are still apt to be more or less regarded as 'cranks', if merely because of their unconventional eating habits.

As to how many doctors also patronize these stores, either in their own interest or that of their patients, there are no statistics to enable one to discover; and anyhow the matter would only be of interest if it served to give some indication of the present attitude on the part of the general medical profession towards the more unusual therapies, of which the subject of this book is one.

As the reader will see, it is concerned with the actual personal experiences of the numerous persons who have resorted to molasses-therapy with such remarkable curative results. Indeed, not long after the first edition of the book was published, I began to receive unsolicited letters to that effect, not only from Britishers but also from people living in various countries abroad. Some of the letters — coming notably from America — were ones asking me whether so-named *blackstrap* molasses sold over there was the same or as good as the *crude black molasses* procurable over here? — to which question I am now able to answer that the difference is solely one of name; a fact I ask my American readers especially to note.

FEATURES OF THE PRESENT EPOCH

We live, one might say, in an era of 'wonder drugs' and patent foods, not to mention the great variety of patent medicines, all of which are doubtless very lucrative propositions, and some of which may be useful to counteract to a certain extent the undesirable effects of a diet deficient in vitamins and mineral tissue-salts. The drugs and even some of the patent foods — as many people may have read in the papers — have acquired for a time a certain delusive reputation, then later fallen into disrepute because in the end some of them have been found to be actually harmful. Even, for instance, the valuable, well known and much prescribed antibiotic *penicillin* has been found to react adversely in a certain number of cases. Is it not significant that out of 350 patients examined by three distinguished doctors of the University of Cincinnati College of Medicine, 16 of those patients reacted unfavourably to *penicillin* — and interesting by the way to note, the men more than the women. Why that should be so was not explained; nor can any explanation be offered in this booklet which, be it emphasized, is neither concerned with a drug nor a fabricated patent food, but with an entirely natural aliment, containing vitamin C and some other elements essential for maintaining bodily health and well-being.

MOLASSES NOT A PATENT FOOD

We live in an age of 'wonder drugs' and patent foods, not to mention the large variety of patent medicines, all of which are very lucrative propositions. Many of the patent foods, mostly sold at health-food stores, are useful to counteract the baneful effects of a diet deficient in vitamins and mineral salts. As for the 'wonder drugs' they have their day and then fall out of repute because, being advertised with a flourish of trumpets, they come to be used indiscriminately, and hence, in many cases, do more harm than good.* Even the use of patent food can be overdone on the assumption that one cannot have too much of a good thing! Yet although I have called molasses a 'wonder food' by way of emphasis there is nothing whatever patent about it, and it can be obtained at most health food stores. I recently wrote a short series of articles in a widely read health magazine, and, judging from the avalanche of letters I received, it seemed desirable and expedient to enlarge on the subject in the form of the present book.

Already, before the First Great War, the late Dr Forbes Ross drew attention to the value of

---

*Doctors Leon Goldman, Forman Friend and Lester M. Mason, of the University of Cincinatti College of Medicine, examined 350 patients and found 16 reacted unfavourably to contact with penicillin, men more than women.

Their article in the journal of the American Medical Association advised, 'use penicillin only where and when indicated . . . not indiscriminately for everything.'

molasses in connection with cancer.† He pointed out that workers on sugar-cane plantations, who were constantly sucking the crude sugar, seldom if ever were known to suffer from the dread disease. He attributed this to the large percentage of potassium salts in unrefined sugar-cane; his contention being that the cause of cancer was a deficiency of potash in the human cells and blood. I have dealt with his contentions in some detail in my earlier books and cannot repeat myself in these pages.* Suffice it to say that although Dr Forbes Ross's numerous cures of cancer, together with the books he wrote on the subject, did not receive at the time the recognition they deserved, several eminent physicians of various schools have since come to uphold his views.

I will now, without further preamble, proceed to deal with the comparatively large number of diseases which have yielded to molasses-therapy.

GROWTHS

That *growths* and the discovery of their cause and cure have for years taxed the ingenuity of a large number of researchers in many countries, is a matter sufficiently well known to need no emphasis here. Nevertheless, despite those years of careful research, the usual treatment would still seem to be either surgery, ray-therapy or sometimes both, which after all only deal with an *effect* but not with the cause, or better said causes, of

†See Appendix.

*see *Doctors, Disease and Health, Victory over Cancer, Health, Diet and Commonsense.*

which there are more than one ... For instance, cases of cancer have been found to occur in workers engaged in certain industries who are obliged to be in almost constant contact with substances proved to contain definitely cancer-producing elements. With such cases, however, this book is not concerned, in that the beneficial effects of the crude black molasses treatment are not derived from any antidoting of pernicious substances — indeed that is not the function of molasses — but by the supplying of the body in a natural, harmless way with those elements essential to prevent the morbid proliferation of any of its cells. And now having drawn attention to this important point, the facts are as follows.

My attention was more fully drawn to the curative and prophylactic elements in crude black molasses by one of my numerous correspondents, Mr James Persson, provision merchant, of Palmerston N., New Zealand. Some years ago Mr Persson was broken in health and unable to do even the lightest work. He was suffering from a growth in the bowels, hardening valves of the heart, blocked bronchial tubes, constipation, indigestion, pyorrhoea, sinus trouble and weak nerves. In addition to this array of symptoms, he was losing weight, and his hair had turned white. Despite consulting doctors and specialists his condition was getting steadily worse. Then one day he heard of Mr S. who happened to be a neighbour of the postman, from whom he got the details I will now mention. Mr S. had suffered from an inoperable growth in the bowels; in other words, he had been opened up by the surgeons, and then stitched up again, his condition being regarded as so hopeless that even the idea of surgical interference was abandoned. Thus, he was discharged from hospital, and only given seven weeks to live. However, he was subsequently induced by an acquaintance to try the effect of taking molasses; with the astonishing result that far from dying within the seven weeks, he finally made a complete recovery. On hearing of this remarkable case, Mr Persson decided to try the treatment himself — and not only did the growth in his bowels disappear, together with all his other troubles (and this after seven years' suffering), but his hair, which was white when he started the treatment, actually regained its original colour and assumed a more healthy appearance in every respect. It should be mentioned that Mr Persson was over sixty at the time.

Having proved for himself the curative value of molasses, he resolved to supply the aliment at a low rate so as to keep down the price, seeing the chemists were selling a *medicated* variety at a much higher figure, and thereby spoiling the substance while pretending to improve it. But I shall have something more to say about this later on. Meanwhile, I should repeat here that Mr Persson's activities were instrumental in bringing him into contact, either directly or indirectly, with a very large number of sufferers from various diseases, including growths. For Mr S's cure, and Mr Persson's own cure having become known, the demand for molasses was such that Mr Persson was at one time supplying a ton of it a month, and later on even more.

As growths are serious conditions for which the orthodox medico generally advises radium or the knife, I am dealing with these in my first section.

Among the numerous cases cured solely by molasses-therapy are growths of the uterus, growths of the breast, further instances of intestinal growth, also numerous cases of growths of the tongue, diagnosed as malignant. One man with a fibroid growth of the tongue was in such a condition that he was unable to speak. But by dint of repeatedly holding molasses in his mouth and also taking it internally the growth came away and the man was cured. And yet this merely bears out the late Dr Forbes Ross's contention that growths of the tongue (he used the word cancer) had been cured by sucking this natural aliment. As for tumours, fibroid growths in various sites of the body, these, according to Mr Persson and to reports received by him, have withered away without any other measures than that of taking molasses internally and using it in the form of poultices.

A recent case of uterine growth may now be mentioned in some detail. The sufferer visited Mr Persson in a very distressed frame of mind. She had been told by the doctors that she was suffering from cancer, and could not be expected to live for more than about six weeks. The diagnosis may have been incorrect, but in any case her doctors took a very serious view of her condition, for she had lost much weight and suffered from severe haemorrhages. Having heard of molasses for growths, she subsequently applied to Mr Persson for a quantity, which she proceeded to take via mouth, and also to use in blood-warm water as a douche. Some months after she had started the treatment she called to see Mr Persson again; and he reports that she was so changed for the better in every way that he could hardly believe it was the same woman. The bleeding had ceased, she had regained her normal weight, her colour was healthy, and she confessed to feeling 'wonderful'.

Here is another case worthy of mention, Mrs. M. had a breast growth. Given two months to live. After employing molasses-therapy, the growth disappeared, and she was perfectly well. Many months elapsed. No recurrence.

Mr Persson writes: 'Many sufferers, after taking molasses for some time, cough up rotten growths.' He then, among others, gives the case of a man said to be suffering from cancer of the gullet. Breath very foul until lately. This unfortunate man had to be fed by means of a tube. He is treating himself with molasses. Has already coughed up 'a rotten lump about the size of a small egg, and his breath does not smell bad any more.' My correspondent adds: 'I have come across some terrible cases, yet wonderful to relate, they have been cured by molasses.'

VARICOSE VEINS

To cure this all too common and unsightly complaint, certain naturopaths in America have for some time been successfully using the molasses treatment. But, although significant that may be, especially significant is an unsolicited letter I received from an old lady in Canada, who informed me she had for fifty-two years suffered from varicose veins, which had become so enlarged that she could not put her legs straight down in bed. The several doctors she had consulted all confessed that they had in their entire practice never seen such veins, and the only thing they could advise was to cut them out. This the old lady 'at *her* age' refused to allow . . . Then one day an acquaintance suggested she might try taking molasses. This she did, though without expecting that it would do any good. The result was that after taking it for a few weeks, she woke up one morning to find to her amazement that the diseased veins had completely disappeared.

ARTHRITIS

There is a reason why this section dealing with arthritis should follow immediately the foregoing one devoted to the cure of varicose veins. That reason is that the writer of the letter previously quoted had prior to taking crude black molasses not only suffered from the exceptionally enlarged veins, but also from extremely painful arthritis. Yet so effective did the treatment prove to be — some doctors declare that arthritis is incurable — that after a little while, she wrote me, her arthritic condition had so improved, she could swing her arms round as fast as any young person; a feat which she demonstrated to her doctor and also to a surgeon, who, although they were obviously surprised, did not see fit to make any comment . . . Nor could they be expected to, considering that for a doctor or a surgeon to admit that anything so simple as molasses could cure such afflictions as those from which the Canadian old lady had suffered, would hardly be consistent with orthodox medical beliefs.

Nevertheless, what are the actual facts? During the years since the book on molasses-therapy was written, so many first-hand reports have been received testifying to its efficacy, that it is only reasonable to adduce them: or at least, so as not to over-extend this book, some of them.

Lady, turned 70. Complete fixation of hip joints for three years. Knees could not be flexed. Much pain and and fatigue. Could only walk painfully with the aid of sticks. Injections given by a doctor, but with no beneficial result. Finally a specialist suggested an operation, but could not guarantee a success. Patient declined the operation, heard of the molasses treatment and decided to try it. Result; in a comparatively short time, she could walk without sticks, and her knees having lost their stiffness, she could even kick her posterior with her heels!

Another case; lady of 40 years of age. Bad arthritis in knees and hip joints. Much pain, was unable to walk without sticks, and she also in a comparatively short time after taking molasses was able to flex her knees and painlessly to swing her legs.

Yet another case, that of an old man. Before taking molasses he had only been able to hobble about with the aid of crutches. But although his cure took longer to achieve than did those previously mentioned, it was achieved in the end.

Venturing to assume that these few very significant cases may suffice to dispel the notion that molasses is far too simple a substance to possess such widely remedial properties, we may now pass on to some other relevant considerations.

In cases where the joints were badly swollen, some doctors who believe in the molasses treatment have found that excellent results may be obtained by bathing them with molasses mixed with creosote; this in addition to taking the pure molasses by mouth.

It is important to mention in this connection that the late Dr Forbes Ross' conclusions agree with those of the naturopaths, i.e., the usual diet of occidentals with its deficiency of those vital biochemic elements so essential to sound health, is to be blamed for the incidence of arthritis and many other chronic disorders. And because crude black molasses supplies those lacking elements in a natural, harmless way, its therapeutical value should be obvious to all open-minded persons. For cases resulting from serious injury, however, it cannot be expected to act as a *cure*: but at least might serve to prevent the victim from eventually becoming arthritic.

It is worthy of note that worry is conducive to arthritis. In fact there are cases where a great shock or worry has caused a relapse. In such cases it is of great importance to continue the treatment, seeing that worry uses up the potassium salts in the blood and tissues, therefore trouble may ensure if these are not replenished. Sugar-cane molasses is here especially important, as the type made from beet sugar is less rich in phosphates, of which, I may add, phosphate of iron is a very valuable one. The reason is that it favours the oxidization of the blood when taken, though not otherwise, in that assimilable form in which only nature supplies it.

ULCERS

People whose blood is in perfect condition do not suffer from ulcers, especially from a chronic state of ulceration. It is true that doctors can usually cure isolated abscesses, on the other hand such afflictions as ulcerated legs have proved very difficult to heal by orthodox medical methods; though I do happen to know of one doctor who has cured hundreds of very bad cases with his own particular methods.* But that is by the way; we are here concerned with ulcers and ulceration cured by no other means than by molasses. A few years ago a certain doctor in New Zealand was so much afflicted with ulcers that his own skill proved insufficient to cure them. In fact, this doctor was very ill and would doubtless have remained so had he not heard of the molasses-treatment and was open-minded enough to try it. The upshot was that after taking molasses for a given period, all his ulcers vanished and he was restored to excellent health.

According to practitioners of the *biochemic system of medicine,* ulcers do not occur unless there is some deficiency of certain mineral salts in the blood and tissues. As molasses, if taken over the requisite time, makes good that deficiency, it is not surprising to hear that *gastric* ulcers have also yielded to the treatment. Indeed the site of the ulcer is not of great importance, seeing that when the blood and tissues are supplied with the essential salts and vitamins to maintain their health, in many cases the local manifestation of the trouble automatically disappears. As all sensible healers know without the telling it is foolish and futile *merely* to treat the local condition — which is only an effect — without removing the prime cause; the untenable supposition being that the

*See *Medicine, Rational and Irrational,* Part II, Chap. VI.

body is not a unity and that the parts can be divided from the whole. The rational method of treatment is, where indicated, to treat both locally and internally, as in the case of external ulcers and also skin diseases, as the following case shows.

DERMATITIS, ECZEMA, PSORIASIS

Mr L. Hands very red and swollen with dermatitis. He was induced to soak his hands frequently in water to which some molasses had been added, and to take molasses several times a day. The cure was complete in six weeks. This is very different from the suppressive treatment which unfortunately many unenlightened skin specialists advocate; their usual procedure being to use ointments which, although they may cure the local condition are apt later on to give rise to something worse — not uncommonly asthma, as many homoeopaths are aware. Seeing that a skin disease is an attempt on the part of nature to rid the body of certain poisons, to suppress that attempt by smearing on ointments is surely to drive those poisons back into the body and so frustrate nature. It would not even be wise merely to apply diluted molasses, despite its healing properties, for it is essential that the patient should take the substance internally at the same time so as to get rid of that condition of the blood and tissues which is primarily responsible for the disorder. Experience over a period of nine years has proved that the molasses-treatment is a rational and natural-scientific method of curing skin diseases. These include dry eczema, weeping eczema, and even some types of psoriasis, when not due to an emotional disturbance.

HIGH BLOOD-PRESSURE, ANGINA PECTORIS, WEAK HEART

High Blood-pressure, according to biochemists of the Dr Schüssler school, is frequently associated with arteriosclerosis, and like most afflictions that are curable at all, is due to a deficiency of certain of the essential mineral salts. But whether the reader is prepared to accept this dictum or not, the fact remains that the most gratifying results have been obtained in many cases by the molasses-treatment plus the juice of one lemon a day. How is this to be accounted for without making too much demand on the reader's credulity? Simply by realizing that the cause of high blood-pressure lies in the fact that the arteries have lost their elasticity and have got hardened and 'blocked', as it were, so that it is difficult for the blood to circulate through them without a much increased effort on the part of the heart. Yet, as we learn from the *Schüssler biochemic system*, they would not lose their elasticity if one or more of the required mineral salts were not lacking to preserve it. These salts being present in molasses, that is why cases of high blood-pressure have been cured by this aliment. Incidentally, though of great importance, molasses contain ingredients which are very strengthening to the heart muscles. Also, it would seem, that it contains anti-spasm ingredients, notably magnesium, seeing that Mr Persson reports cases of angina pectoris being cured by the treatment. As for weak heart, it has been known for a long time by orthodox doctors (though they often forget it) that brown sugar is good for that condition. But crude black molasses is far superior to ordinary sugar for the purpose because of the concentration of mineral salts which it contains.

Mr Persson reports the case of a number of men who were not granted licences to drive their cars owing to 'bad hearts'. After taking molasses for six weeks they were cured, and able to obtain their licences. Even 'hopeless' cases have recovered, as, for instance, a Mr K., who was in such a condition that his doctor said he might live at the most a week. In fact the physicians had intimated that 'nothing more could be done for him.' Nevertheless after taking molasses for a time he made a complete recovery — a matter which was considered 'an absolute miracle'!

Since writing the above, reports of several gratifying cases in England have come to hand, from which the following may be selected. Lady, aged 63. For some three to four years had suffered from various ailments, and particularly from recurrent heart attacks. The patient would wake in the night with violent palpitation, pain, a feeling of suffocation and fright. The face was hot and flushed. Her doctor prescribed remedies, which gave temporary relief but failed to effect a cure. The patient was growing more and more depressed and dissatisfied with life. She was then sent a copy of the first edition of this book, and contrived to obtain some molasses. After taking it for several weeks, I received a grateful letter from her saying that she 'felt an entirely different woman.' No more malaise, no more heart attacks. A further letter from her after several months had passed reported that there had been no return of the trouble. She continued to take the molasses and was so pleased with the results that she was recommending the treatment to all her ailing friends. Similar cases could be cited did space permit.

I will conclude this section with a brief mention of a case of cardiac thrombosis (blood clot). The sufferer was a railway worker who had been obliged to give up his job for life owing to his condition. He was induced to try the molasses and was so pleased with the results that he was able to go back to work — a fit man. The potassium and other mineral salts in the aliment had dispersed the clot. I may add that potassium is one of the chief salts used by biochemic practitioners for the cure of thrombosis. (See *Appendix* for a further case.)

CONSTIPATION, COLITIS

Constipation is the bugbear of civilization, and a goldmine to the manufacturing chemists. The obvious reason is that the bulk of people live on deficiency foods, or what the Americans call processed foods; moreover the advent of the motor-car has caused people to take less exercise. Consequently the chemists advertise hundreds of different kinds of laxatives, and the health-food manufacturers sell quantities and varieties of cereals (in packets) calculated to move the bowels. These are well enough in their way, and useful to counteract the bad effects of deficiency flour; but if it were made compulsory — which God forbid — for people to eat whole-meal bread complete with the wheat germ, these 'packet-foods' would be superfluous; nor would I need to draw attention to molasses as a mild and natural evacuent, which undoubtedly it is.

We are told nowadays that constipation comes

from an insufficient amount of bulk and roughage, which dictum is only a half-truth, for a great deal of costiveness comes from the fact that the bowels have lost tone because they have not been supplied with the necessary mineral salts to cause them to function properly. And here is where molasses proves so valuable, for the salts it contains help to re-establish muscular tone if taken sufficiently to effect this desideratum. This does not mean that molasses will cure every case of constipation, especially if sufferers live and have lived for years on a 'rubbishy' diet of white bread, meat and boiled vegetables of which all the valuable salts have been thrown down the sink. In such cases other measures are required — not purgatives which make matters worse the longer they are resorted to, but measures which are natural as opposed to medicinal i.e., assist nature in a mechanical manner without producing offensive manifestations. To be explicit: all that is needed is a teaspoonful of linseed, or even a little more if necessary. These seeds should be washedthrough a sieve or tea-strainer, then swallowed with a little water. Their action is twofold; they swell and produce bulk, and at the same time the oil is liberated and acts as a natural and harmless lubricant. As linseed is no more a poison to human beings than canary seed is a poison to canaries, it can be taken every night without the least harm. In any event, where indicated, it should be taken for at least a month, in that its good effects are cumulative.

I mention this harmless evacuent because if people who are treating themselves with molasses, say, for heart trouble, imagine they can at the same time wisely take their daily dose of liquid paraffin

— that being the fashion at present — they are mistaken, the reason being, that medicinal paraffin is apt to interfere with the absorption of certain vitamins, and some doctors even go so far as to say it interferes with the absorption of one's food in general.

The value of black treacle as a mild aperient has been recognized by homoeopaths for a long time. The *modus operandi* is to dissolve a teaspoonful of it in a tumbler of water, then sip it while dressing in the morning. Nevertheless crude black molasses is far superior to black treacle for the purpose of producing an evacuation. In obstinate cases a dessertspoonful, or even a tablespoonful, should be taken in warm water, on rising, in addition to the daily doses with meals. The practice should be kept up for four to six weeks to effect the cure.

Colitis is another disease of so-called civilization; though admittedly the name is used to cover a variety of conditions — such as diarrhoea of old people. Reports are to hand of cases cured by taking molasses internally and using enemas in the following way.

Melt a teaspoonful of molasses in warm water, then add 3 pts. of water so that the temperature of the enema be blood-heat. To obtain the best effects, enemata may be taken every day for the first week, every other day the second week, and every two days the third week. Then discontinued; *except in cases of bowel-growths,* where persistence may be necessary. (See *Appendix.*)

STROKES

According to 'the biochemic system of medicine,'

the majority of diseases that are curable at all, are simply due to a deficiency of certain of the mineral salts. It is therefore no surprise to students of this system that many strokes have yielded to molasses-therapy, seeing that the aliment is so especially rich in a variety of these mineral salts. Where paralysis is exhibited, unless due to accident, there is a lack of calcium, potassium and magnesium in the body; and all these salts are present in assimilable form in crude black molasses.

Now the general supposition is that when a person has had two strokes, the third one will kill him or her, as the case may be. And yet it need not be so, or at any rate not invariably, as the following brief case-history reveals. Mr. X, an elderly man, suffered two strokes and was completely paralysed down one side of his body. He then tried molasses-therapy – with the gratifying result that he *recovered the use of all his limbs,* and became completely fit, much to the astonishment of his doctor and his friends. Nor is this by any means an isolated case, and if I have selected it out of many others, it is because it happens to be a particularly bad one.

The question of paralytic strokes gives one much food for reflection, and I think it is not going too far to say that if people would make molasses a part of their daily diet there might be fewer cases of this dreadful affliction.

SOME MISCELLANEOUS CASES

(1) A boy who had been very dull and backward mentally, was put on to the molasses-treatment by his father. He is now as bright and healthy as the

rest of the family.

(2) An X-ray photograph revealed that a certain man had a patch on his lung. He was induced to try molasses, and after taking it for a given period was X-rayed a second time: the radiograph showed a complete disappearance of the patch.

(3) A Maori girl was said by the doctors to be suffering from tuberculosis of the lung. But whether the diagnosis was correct, or not, she was undoubtedly in very poor health. After taking a course of molasses, her health was restored to normality.

(4) A man was in much pain with a *poisoned finger*. He also had a lump under his arm. The poisoned finger was treated locally with molasses compresses, and healed in three days. The lump under his arm vanished as the result of taking molasses internally.

(5) Cases of *sinus trouble* have yielded to the treatment in a most gratifying manner. For this complaint, the substance must be taken internally, and a mild solution of it (proportions the same as for an enema) used as a nasal douche. The same measures have also been found very beneficial in cases of nasal catarrh. Antrum trouble should also be mentioned in this connection.

(6) Mr Persson reports a case of *erysipelas* cured with molasses; and the doctor in attendance advised the patient to continue taking the aliment in view of its beneficial result.

(7) Before Mr Persson took molasses, he was suffering from pyorrhoea, as already stated. Pyorrhoea is a constitutional disease with local manifestation. The doctors advocate extraction of the teeth so as to liberate the poisons, but the real

cause of the trouble lies in a deficiency of certain of the mineral salts, hence molasses-therapy is more rational and less expensive, and should be tried before drastic measures are adopted. Molasses diluted should be used as a mouthwash as well as taken internally in the prescribed manner. As an adjunct to the treatment the biochemic cell-salts, *Kali mur.*, *Calc. flour*, *Nat. phos.*, all in the 6*x* potency can be taken in a combination tablet (three tablets twice daily). When improving, then *Calc sulph.* 6*x* and *Silica* 12*x* can be taken concurrently (E. F. W. Powell, D.Sc.).

ANAEMIA, PERNICIOUS ANAEMIA
Considering the amount of assimilable iron and calcium in molasses, it is not surprising to hear that many cases of anaemia have been cured by taking the aliment. The orthodox treatment of anaemia, which consists largely in the administration of some preparation of iron in large doses for a long time, is not only unsatisfactory but is often attended with unpleasant results in the form of digestive disturbances. The reason is obvious to all naturopaths, for iron and calcium should be absorbed from some natural food and not from some medicinal preparation, however scientific it is supposed to be. As for that grievous form of anaemia known as *pernicious* anaemia, I was not at all astonished to hear that it also had yielded to molasses therapy and that Mr Persson was able to report quite a number of cures. Indeed, I hardly expected otherwise, considering some years ago I heard from a lady correspondent that she had been entirely cured of pernicious anaemia by taking, on

the advice of a 'quack', a dessert-spoonful of black treacle twice daily. As, however, crude black molasses contains a greater concentration of mineral salts than black treacle, theoretically I argued that it should prove even more effective. Thereafter came the reports showing that the theory had proved correct.

BLADDER TROUBLES, DIFFICULT URINATION

And apropos of theories: as molasses has been shown to diminish growths, cause them to drop off, or make them automatically disappear, there is good reason to suppose that the potassium salts in molasses should prevent or cure prostatic enlargement in elderly men. But although there are cases to hand of bladder trouble and difficult urination, as Mr Persson is not a doctor and doesn't profess to be one, the exact nature of these cases has not been specified. Nevertheless, some of them do suggest prostate troubles, as, for instance, the following old man. Great difficulty in urinating. Was about to enter hospital because of stoppage. Was then urged to take molasses, and also to chew plenty of parsley. Result — he finally got well and did not have to go into hospital. Other cases of bladder trouble (though they may not have been connected with the prostate) have yielded to molasses-therapy combined with the imbibing of plenty of parsley juice or parsley water.

GALL-STONES

There is a treatment for gall-stones, which consists in taking molasses in the prescribed manner plus

3-4 teaspoonfuls of olive oil every day. This treatment is not so far-fetched as may appear on the surface, considering that copper and several of the other minerals to be found in molasses are used by biochemists of the Schüssler school as remedies for this agonizing condition. As to the olive oil its function is obvious. But were I personally afflicted with gall-stones I should be more inclined to use 'Dutch drops', otherwise known as oil of Haarlem* in place of the olive oil; and this because I have known Dutch drops to cure gall-stones after a variety of treatments had been previously and unsuccessfully tried. It is very probable, however, that molasses would enhance the treatment. It is also probable that the inclusion of Molasses in one's daily diet would act as a preventive.

NERVE CASES

The effects of the molasses-therapy on bad nerves and war-neurosis have been so pronounced that the wives of soldiers returned from the war have noticed the striking improvement in their husbands and have expressed their gratitude for all that molasses has done for these unfortunate sufferers. As for nervous children, they have benefited so greatly that whole families are now being given daily doses of the aliment as an adjunct to their diet. The treatment has not only benefited their nerves but has also made them healthier and stronger in every way.

*Oil of Haarlem consists of sulphurated oil with a little refined turpentine.

PREGNANCY, CHANGE OF LIFE

Many prospective mothers who have been advised to take molasses during the term of pregnancy have not only had easy confinements but have given birth to unusually healthy infants.

The menopause is said to be, and often *is*, a very difficult time with women. But this, in a large number of cases, must be attributed to years of wrong feeding, and a deficiency of mineral salts and vitamins. It is, therefore, not surprising to hear that the molasses-treatment has proved of enormous value to women at this critical period of their lives.

UNHEALTHY FINGER NAILS, THE HAIR

Dr Forbes Ross, in his book on cancer, mentioned the beneficial effect of potassium salts on brittle and crumbling finger nails. Similar effects have been observed after taking molasses for even a week or two; brittle or crumbling nails having regained their firmness. There is also, in many cases, a noticeable improvement in the hair; a fact which Dr Forbes Ross likewise mentioned in connection with his potassium treatment.* Some women who had been prematurely grey, were even wrongly accused of resorting to hair-dye, seeing that their hair had regained its original colour. Indeed the fact that the taking of molasses should in some instances restore the pigment of the hair opens up a new field for speculation and investigation as to the real cause of premature greyness — unless attributable to shock or intense grief. For it shows that grey hair must be primarily due to a

*See *Appendix* 1, para. 2; also *Appendix* II.

lack of some particular ingredient in the human body, an ingredient which is present in molasses. To assume, however, that the missing ingredient was potassium alone would not be safe, in that molasses contains other salts; and so did the Forbes Ross formula for growths — it contained, among other things, a certain small percentage of iron, though he considered the potash the most important . . . But I will not enlarge on this matter.

THE EFFECT OF MOLASSES AFTER OR BEFORE SURGICAL INTERFERENCE

A man with a large lump below the knee (diagnosed as cancer) decided to have it extirpated. But prior to the operation he was induced to take a course of the molasses-treatment. The subsequent speedy and perfect healing of the wound was commented on by his physicians. This is no isolated case. Mr Persson informs me that judging from many reliable reports received, the evidence goes to show that when surgery has been resorted to for one reason or another, the healing processes have been much facilitated and accelerated when the patient has taken a course of molasses prior to and following the operation.

'PREVENTION IS BETTER THAN CURE'

The truth of this hackneyed old saying has been twisted and exploited for insidious commercial purposes on the disregarded assumption that one can 'prevent' a thing which nobody can be certain is bound to occur. This would not matter much if the alleged preventives were entirely harmless. But unfortunately many of the vaccines and serums now used in orthodox medicines have in a number of cases either immediate or long-delayed after-effects of a harmful nature. The trouble is, however, that just as it is impossible to prove save by circumstantial evidence that so-termed prophylactics do not prevent what might never have happened in any case, so it is impossible to prove save by circumstantial evidence their long-delayed undesirable after-effects. For instance, I recently heard from a naturopath in Australia that since an increasing number of children in that continent have been immunized against diphtheria, there has been a considerable increase in cases of infantile paralysis among the child population. Now it is a significant fact that immunization in many isolated cases has been known to cause paralysis, sometimes lasting for a whole week in the newly immunized. This being the case, can it be ruled out that instead of paralysis occuring immediately, and eventually passing off, the action of the serum may be delayed and give rise at a later date to that more intractable form termed infantile paralysis?

Now, crude black molasses being a perfectly natural aliment has no harmful after-effects. Wisely did that excellent homoeopath, Dr Dorothy Shepherd, who wrote many enlightening books, give utterance to the dictum; 'let your foods be your medicines' — which also means your prophylactics. But this wise injunction is far from being generally heeded by the community at large.

MOLASSES COULD SOLVE THE PROBLEM
How, then, is the problem to be solved? If people

will not or cannot live on a well-balanced diet, which, as every naturopath knows, is the secret of health provided there is no interference from disruptive emotions, then the best thing to do is to consume as a daily habit at least one food which contains the largest proportion of essentials to keep the blood and cells in a healthy condition, thus acting as a prophylaxis against the chronic disorders enumerated in these pages. From what has already been written it will have become obvious that the food in question is crude black molasses. In addition to its other valuable salts content, cane-sugar molasses contains 700 international units per hundred (approximately 3½ ounces) of Vitamin B_2. As for the mineral salts, a rough analysis of one specimen used in this country for making silage, revealed 9 per cent of these necessary substances. The percentage, however, is probably higher in the molasses obtained from Jamaica for the same purpose and for the therapeutical purposes to which my correspondent, Mr Persson, has drawn attention.

It may be asked, is it to be inferred that I am going so far as to maintain that molasses will prevent smallpox, typhoid, diphtheria and all the other acute diseases which vaccines are said to prevent? Yet granted that acute diseases are much less likely to occur when the blood and tissues are kept in a healthy state through absorbing the requisite vitamins and mineral salts, the type of prevention with which we are here concerned is of quite a different order. To illustrate my point I will again refer to Dr Forbes Ross, and at this juncture, to his noteworthy experience in connection with cancer. For during the whole of his years of practice he noticed that not one of his many regular patients ever developed malignancy; and he attributed this to the fact that he freely used potassium in his prescriptions, a policy which no other doctor, to his knowledge, had adopted. Here then we have, not the proof, but at any rate circumstantial evidence that potassium salts prevent cancer.

WHITE SUGAR: ACID FORMING MOLASSES: ALKALINE ACTION

I shall be doing no damage to the white sugar industry when I voice the dictum of food chemists that white sugar tends to create acidity; for just as people *will* eat white bread (when they can get it), so will they eat white sugar in preference to brown, however much they may be told that the latter is much more salubrious. Nor will they refrain from eating white sugar when they are told that it is conducive to rheumatism and distinctly bad for the teeth, as opposed to molasses which tends to preserve the teeth, and, having a somewhat alkaline action, helps to ward off rheumatism and even to cure it. Furthermore, far from containing a harmful 'bug,' it has been shown to contain a germicide which destroys harmful bacteria in the intestinal tract. These facts having been put forward by food chemists and food specialists, the rational thing to do is to mix a little molasses with all our jams and marmalade, just as an artist mixes his medium with his paints. In other words, white sugar having been deprived of its most essential and wholesome elements, these should be put back in the manner indicated above.

MOLASSES AND THE NATIONAL HEALTH

It may also be argued that in drawing attention to an aliment which possesses such extensive prophylactic and curative elements, I am thereby doing a disservice to the medical profession. But, on the contrary, I hope I am doing its overworked members a distinct service. Unless the national health, especially among the working classes, is reasonably sound, the policy of turning the doctors into civil servants will simply result in their being terribly overworked. Therefore, it is in the interest of doctors that the food of the community should be as health-promoting as possible. To this end the Ministry of Health should see to it that all such food is available, as it is in Australia, New Zealand, Canada, America, and other countries that could be mentioned. It is interesting to note that in Palmerston, N.Z., where Mr Persson had for nine years been supplying large quantities of molasses of the best and crudest kind, the latest statistics recorded a lower death rate and a greater population.

SUGAR CANE: A LIFE-SUSTAINING FOOD IN ITSELF

The following information was given to me by a lady who has recently returned from India, where an associate of hers owned a cane-sugar plantation. She told me that some of the workers in the plantation were so poor, and that food was at times so scarce, that they were obliged to live on and to feed their children on sugar-cane exclusively. They ate all but the fibres, which they ejected; and on this mono-diet contrived to sustain life and remain healthy.

METHOD OF TAKING MOLASSES

Molasses may be taken at any time whenever most convenient; before, during or after meals according to individual inclination. There is no set rule. The dosage is one teaspoonful, which should be dissolved in half a cup of hot water, then cold water should be added, so as to make two-thirds of a cupful, the latter to be drunk warm. For children, half the dosage. The molasses *can* be taken neat; but hot water should be drunk immediately afterwards. Some people, however, find the latter method unsuited to them. The patient must use his own judgment and adapt the method to his individual taste. Persons with delicate stomachs who find a teaspoonful too much at one time, should take a smaller dose but more often during the day. In severe cases, such as for growth, molasses should be taken last thing at night and on rising, as well as during the day. The water should of course never be too hot; never hotter than a temperature in which one can comfortably bear to put one's finger. It is the utmost folly to drink any beverage scaldingly hot, like some persons drink tea. Another point is that the molasses-and-water mixtures should not be gulped down like nasty medicine so as to produce flatulence, but should be sipped and tasted like connoisseurs taste good wines. The reason for taking the molasses in hot water is because by being thus diluted it is more easily assimilated, and also more digestible. Cold water with some people is apt to chill the stomach. Even bladder troubles can occur after people have drunk draughts of cold water at a time when they are over-heated.

Both children and adults can, if preferred, take

molasses in the milk they use with their porridge or dry cereals for breakfast or at other times. I have already mentioned how a little molasses may be and should be mixed with marmalade and all jams made from white sugar. I have also mentioned how molasses should be taken per rectum in cases of growths in the bowels, or colitis, etc. For external growths, boils, sores, cuts, etc., molasses mixed with water should be applied as a poultice, in addition to the internal treatment. As a natural ointment molasses has no equal.

In this connection the following is of interest; an ex-soldier wrote to me saying that in the first world war he had sustained a wound in the leg, which absolutely refused to heal. Then after more than thirty years of suffering, he heard of molasses, applied it to the wound and took it internally. Result — complete healing in a very short time. As the reader will have gleaned, the various methods of taking molasses are quite simple. But of course it is important to take the most suitable kind. It is unwise to take any *medicated* or *sulphured* aliment over a long period, indeed, if at all, according to naturopaths. And hence a brand of pure, chemically-untampered-with molasses is the one to use . . . And by the way, some people in this country (England) have rather vague notions as to what the name molasses really denotes. Many individuals seem to think it is a synonym for black treacle. This, however, is incorrect, or at best misleading. The 'Universal English Dictionary' defines the aliment as 'the thick, non-crystallizable dark syrup which drains from raw sugar during manufacture; thickest kind of treacle.' Nevertheless, ordinary black treacle is not molasses, good though it is, for the reason that it is not the *thickest* kind; it is much richer in sugar than the type of molasses most suited for therapeutical purposes.

Some stoutish people have complained that molasses has increased their weight. When this has happened, the dosages should consist of less molasses but more diluted, and they should be taken less often. In some cases recourse to the Cider Vinegar treatment should prove effective. (See book entitled 'Cider Vinegar'.)

Also, some people complain that certain brands sold in the shops are so sweet and sickly that they cannot bring themselves to take any of them. And yet the right sort of molasses for remedial purposes should not be sickly sweet.

WARNING

Diabetes is one of those diseases for which molasses therapy is not suitable, and diabetics should not take molasses. Sufferers would be well advised to consult a homoeopathic doctor or a practitioner of the biochemic system of medicine.

CONCLUSION

It may be thought that I have made too many claims for this 'wonder-food,' so I will conclude with a note of warning. That great German naturopath, Louis Kuhne, maintained that he could cure all diseases with his therapy but that he *could not cure all patients.* His meaning should become obvious as soon as we reflect that to say we cure a disease is only a half-truth, for what we really mean is that we cure an individual ... or should do, if we are not incompetent bunglers and he is curable at all. Now not only are no claims made that molasses-therapy can cure every disease, but no claim is even made that it can cure all patients suffering from the disorders mentioned in these pages. If a patient resorts to molasses-therapy when it is already too late, it stands to reason that he cannot be cured. Nevertheless, numerous patients have been restored to health by this natural and harmless means when orthodox methods have entirely failed. Many letters have been received from grateful erstwile sufferers — among them doctors and clergymen — saying that 'since taking molasses I am an entirely new man.' The reason is obvious to students of biochemistry and dietetics; such people having fed on deficiency foods have then taken molasses and thereby, perhaps for the first time in their lives, have supplied the essential elements which their bodies needed. All the same, if they discontinue taking molasses, they are likely in the course of time to suffer again, for potassium salts are the salts in particular which require constant replenishing, moreover, as biochemists point out, they are the most soluble salts (especially pot. phos.), and are easily lost when foods are cooked or boiled. Hence the advisability of taking molasses, let us say, about once a day even after good health has been established. This is all the more imperative, because, in addition to the deficiency diet on which the majority of people live, the consumption of salty and soda-impregnated foods has vastly increased of late years. To this fact Dr Henty Smalpage (Australia) attributes the much greater prevalence of tumours, cysts and cancerous growths. His contentions in his book on *Cancer*, if considered in conjunction with those of the late Dr Forbes Ross, are highly significant. If the sodium salts absorbed from soda-impregnated foods in far too large quantities, and also the table salt used as a condiment, are not counteracted by potassium salts constantly replenished, there is the liability of growths or arthritis developing. The reason is that all this unusable amount of soda is not eliminated via the kidneys but manifests as a 'lump' in some people or as that debilitating condition termed rheumatoid arthritis. Potassium salts, however, effect this elimination and thus the danger is greatly minimized.

The most natural way of getting these salts into the system is by taking crude black molasses.

NOTE: Further significant case-histories have come to hand. Here is an arthritis case. Gentleman; in bed for three months with rheumatoid arthritis of such severity that he could hardly move his arms and hands. After having fifty electric and thermal treatments, he was informed that nothing more could be done for him. He then started molasses-therapy, with the result that after 3-4 months his health is in so far normal that he merely experiences slight twinges of pain in wet weather. Another report which has come to hand is that of a lady, whose state was so serious, that after resorting to molasses — so my informant wrote — 'she seems to be arising practically from a condition leading to death . . .'

APPENDIX 1
Extracts from the late Dr Forbes Ross's book
Cancer: Its Cause and Cure, long out of print.

(1) 'The negroes of the West Indies on sugar plantations who have in the past shown a singular immunity from cancer, have always been most prodigious consumers of crude sugar. Crude sugar contains a large proportion of potassium salts, which for the most part is removed from the white or refined article. Being convinced from experience that the alkaline balance was really a matter of the amount of potassium present in the blood, I proceeded to work on the lines of taking care of the potassium supply of the body and leaving the sodium, calcium and magnesium to look after themselves, because whatever happened their supply at any time would be kept up by food and drink, so that it was only necessary to attend to the supply of the one drug which was likely to vary in quantity to the other salts in the body, that salt being potassium.'*

(2) 'We will now consider the action of

*With all due respects to Dr Forbes Ross, it is doubtful whether the majority of people do absorb a sufficiency of calcium and magnesium salts from the foods they eat, hence they would be well advised to include molasses in their daily diet, seeing it is not only rich in potassium salts but also in calcium, magnesium and iron; in a word, it is the 'perfect food.'

potassium on the hair. If an elderly person, suffering from gout, failure of the heart, or cancer, be made for a certain length of time, say six weeks, to artificially take into his or her body, a definite and ordered amount of potassium, the following changes in the hair will certainly take place. If the hair be previously grey or iron grey it will become generally darker. The first localities of the scalp which will be found to show this change, in white or grey hair, will be a darkening of colour on the temples and the nape of the neck. These preliminary changes will be followed by the appearance of some normally coloured new hairs throughout the whole extent of the scalp, with the exception of those parts which had ceased to have any hair bulbs from which hair could possibly grow. So striking is the change that many elderly lady patients have been accused by their friends and relations of resorting to artifice to produce the resultant darkening and hair rejuvenescence as a result of taking potassium salts.'

'The next point was that at first the scales which were removable from the skin of the body by friction with the hands or towel after the bath, were at first increased in quantity, and then occurred a gradual diminution of the total amount of epithelial scales lost from the surface of the skin, which then gradually sank to only that loss associated with younger persons.'

' . . . The therapeutic agent that will cure cancer will be an agent which forms a natural constituent of the body in health, and therefore one which the body under conditions of disease will make use of to return to conditions of health. The body can only make use naturally of a natural means or force to effect the spontaneous cure of any disease. No medicinal treatment known to man is ever successful unless the body makes use of one of its natural means as the result of that medicinal treatment in order to return to a healthy condition. No disease, whether spontaneously cured or by means of drugs, ever recovers except by reason of the natural forces and constituents of the body . . .'

(3) **Coronary Thrombosis.** Case reported by a doctor. The patient, after being sent to a specialist, was told in effect that he must resign himself to living the life of a mollusc for the rest of his days, and must never do any more work. He finally tried the molasses treatment, which cured him completely, and he was able to resume his job . . I am aware that nowadays certain medicaments are used to treat thrombosis, but have heard that they are apt to make the patients feel so wretched for a while.

(4) **Constipation.** Report from a correspondent. Lady suffered from such obstinate constipation over a great many years that she ruined her health by taking every sort of purgative. She then was urged to try the molasses therapy, which not only cured her constipation but also restored her to excellent health.

(5) Strokes are apt to occur when there is a congestion in the neck. To prevent them, it is a wise practice firmly and often to massage the back and sides of the neck. If obstinate headaches are suffered from, a competent osteopath should be consulted.

APPENDIX II

As according to analysis, molasses contains pantothenic acid, some further reflections on this factor of the Vitamin B complex may prove instructive. Pantothenic acid (as the name implies) is widely distributed in both the vegetable and animal kingdoms. It has sometimes been called 'yeast-growth substance.' or 'chick-antidermatitis factor'; and when there is a deficiency of it in the animal organism, skin, feathers, hair, as also the gastro-intestinal and respiratory systems are adversely affected. In rats the deficiency leads to the greying of the fur, and in mice to baldness. After using synthetic pantothenic acid, plus some other ingredients, on human subjects, certain American researchers noticed such effects as growth of new hair, a more healthy and lustrous appearance of the hair together with a tendency towards a reversion to its original colour. Thus it would seem that pantothenic acid acts to some extent as a 'hair restorer.' But if so, it is not exclusively the pantothenic acid, seeing that before this substance was discovered, grey hair in some cases reverted to its original colour as the result of taking potassium, in accordance with Dr Forbes Ross's formula. And so where molasses has likewise acted as a natural hair restorer, it is not unreasonable to assume that the effect has been produced by the combination of potassium and pantothenic acid, whilst probably the iron and copper in crude black molasses have also been contributing factors.

It is interesting to note that, according to a brief report in the J.A.M.A. (24th November, 1945), Dr W. Stepp, of Munich, had been successfully employing synthetic pantothenic for chronic bronchitis. But, as the late Dr Clarke, of Edinburgh, wrote some years ago, vitamins, etc., should be absorbed from the foods we eat. Dame Nature is a better chemist than the scientist!

ANALYSIS OF SUGAR BEET MOLASSES (IRISH)

Water	21.9%
Albuminoids	10.5%
Carbohydrates	60.4%
Ash	7.2%

100% Starch Eq. 48.

Rich in potassium. Poor in lime and phosphates.